Cheers and Tears

A Collection of True
Animal Stories

Jessica Montgomery

VANTAGE PRESS
New York

FIRST EDITION

Published by Vantage Press, Inc.
419 Park Ave. South, New York, NY 10016

Manufactured in the United States of America
ISBN: 978-0-533-16231-4

Library of Congress Catalog Card No: 2009903866

0 9 8 7 6 5 4 3 2 1

To my late husband, Robert, who was always coming through the door with something.

Cheers and Tears

Contents

Acknowledgments

Page a Day Calendar
M. Piazza

Introduction

I have lived in this house some thirty-five years now and I have watched many animals come and go through my door. Some of those animals I kept for my own, some I found homes for, and some I could not save.

This book is a tribute to all those little creatures.

*   *   *

Goldfinger

My late husband was a big man, gruff and mean looking, with a tender heart of gold. He was always coming through the door with something: an injured bird, a mistreated or handicapped animal, or one he was very simply going to find a home for.

God help me. I was the nurse!

I will start with the most recent hair-raising story, which involved a beautiful golden (salmon-colored) Manx kitten, male. I received a telephone call from my local pet store informing me that they had a gold Manx kitten. I burned the road up getting there and adopted this little guy on the spot. He was so small that he fit in my one hand. He weighed in at one whole pound at the veterinarian's office. That's right, sixteen ounces! I named him Goldfinger. He liked to sit, perfectly balanced, on my left shoulder. His wet nose tickled my neck like a dangle earring. He purred in my ear. Goldfinger was neutered immediately and I did not agree with this. The vet began to give him shots. He gained a pound and now he weighed two pounds.

Then, things started to go wrong. Goldfinger stopped eating and he lost weight. He no longer ran across the yard when I called him. He stayed in the sunspots as if he were cold and his left eye swelled as if it would bulge out of his head. I returned him to the vet. Goldfinger was diagnosed with feline infectious perontonitis (FIP). This is a fatal disease. The vet did not put him to sleep. I left the office at approximately 1:30 P.M. As the day wore on Goldfinger got worse, and at midnight I made an emergency trip to a different veterinarian—a woman. We immediately put Goldfinger to sleep and now the real story begins:

I had chosen to work Christmas Eve and Christmas day to earn money for Goldfinger's cremation. Although I was very busy, there was this funny little tickle on the left side of my neck. It was getting worse and worse and finally, I went and looked in the mirror. Nothing was there, not a strand of hair, nor an insect bite, not even a rash. NOTHING! NOTHING! NOTHING!

Must be dry skin, so I put some hand lotion on it. This funny little tickle that had started Christmas Eve, got worse and worse and aggravated me all through Christmas. The day after Christmas it was gone. As mysteriously as it came, it left.

Now, I'm not one for believing in ghosts, but that funny little tickle was located in the same spot on my neck where Goldfinger used to sit.

Today, Goldfinger's little coffin is proudly kept in my front room and I wear a locket with his photographs in it.

I am honored and thankful that God chose me to care for him for his short period of time on earth.

God bless little Goldfinger.

*　　*　　*

Joe

My husband had retired, and one of his goals was to fish during a weekday off our local wharf. Monday, he was out there at the crack of dawn along with the pelicans, seals, ducks, and all the rest of the unmentionable pests! All he wanted to do was fish. He had saved animals all his life and was now sixty-five years old and wanted a bit of rest from it all.

Fat chance!

What could happen on the wharf? How could a sick or injured animal find his way to the wharf? All we had out here were seals, ducks, and pelicans. He had set up his bait bucket, cast his line in the water, and then sat down on his rickety old lawn chair. The pelicans were flying over that morning, but that was nothing unusual . . . until one landed and started thumping down the wharf . . . right straight towards my husband. He only had one leg and at first my husband thought he was just another beggar.

Although there were many other fishermen on the wharf, strangely, the pelican thumped his way up to my husband. It was only then that Robert saw, in fact, that this pelican had two legs. His second leg was all wound up in fishing line flush against his body and virtually imbedded in his feathers. My husband had never seen such a gnarled, tangled mess of fishing line in all his life. It pinned his leg hopelessly against his body.

4

Robert Jones with Joe the pelican

The line he cast in the water was momentarily forgotten, and Robert got his ever so sharp little pocket knife out. He cut and cut and cut the gnarled fishing line but each and every time was met by more knots. This was going to take time. The pelican got fidgety, and after about fifteen minutes, my husband turned him loose. He didn't know if he would ever see him again. The next morning . . . the pelican was there when my husband drove up, almost as if he were waiting for him.

My husband got his bait bucket, carefully purchasing more than necessary so that Joe (as he was named) could eat also. Again, my husband cut more and more fishing line out of Joe's leg. When Joe became fidgety, my husband would let him go. This became a daily ritual, meeting Joe in the morning, feeding him some fish, and cutting knots out until, one day, his leg started to loosen up a bit. Two weeks had gone by and my husband thought he had all the gnarled fishing line cut out; but Joe's leg did not come down. So my husband pulled on it a little bit and Joe winced in pain. Joe's leg had been tied up so long that he couldn't bring it down. Robert knew at that point it would take a long time to restore Joe's leg before he could use it again.

Therapy and massage were started, and Joe seemed not only to like it but it also gave him a chance to steal extra bites out of my husband's bait bucket. This was an expensive bird.

The months went by and very gradually Joe's leg started to come back. At first, it started to just droop down without any control of movement. Then Joe started to move his leg but still could not use it. The leg hung half way down by now.

Three months had gone by. One morning, Joe came thumping down the deck with his leg swinging forward and backward as if he were trying to walk. He stole his usual breakfast of fish, my husband massaged his leg, pulled it down a little bit more, and let him go.

Many more months went by, and finally Joe's leg was almost touching the ground. One day it did and everybody on the wharf cheered. At first, he walked with a limp, but then Joe was finally able to walk on both feet. The marks of the fishing line never went away.

My husband would fish almost every morning in the wharf after that and would always watch over Joe and give him treats. This friendship lasted until the day my beloved husband passed away.

God bless Joe. He will never be forgotten.

Robert's wish was to be cremated. I chose to bury him at sea, and now another shocking story begins:

I chartered a boat and invited only immediate family members. This gave us a grand total of ten people on the boat (including the captain and first mate). Ten witnesses to the shocking phenomenon that was about to happen.

The fog was so thick that morning that you could not see the pier as we left. Only a small black dot was visible, and that was a tiny black bird perched on an old post. The farther out in the ocean we went, the thicker the fog got until we couldn't see at all. We got to the spot where the ashes were to be placed and my son-in-law performed the ceremony. My husband had been laid to rest.

Out of the fog came four figures, large birds, pelicans! Two birds flew horizontally and the other two flew vertically. They crossed at the exact spot where we had buried my husband. The pelicans flew with the speed, skill, and accuracy of the Blue Angels. As quickly as they had made the "cross" over my husband's ashes, they were gone.

I was numb—to say the least. I couldn't speak; I couldn't cry. I couldn't do anything. I heard my late husband's sister say: "My God, did you see that?! They crossed over the spot where Robert's ashes were."

Yes, I saw it and I will never forget it. I don't believe anybody on that boat will . . . ever.

I know in my heart that one of those pelicans was Joe. God bless Joe. He will never be forgotten.

*　　*　　*

Tripod

The word *tripod* as defined by Webster's Dictionary is "... a three-legged stand for a camera or surveying instrument, etc."

Yes, we have a camera and also a three-legged stand in our house; but this story is not about that camera or its stand. As you might well have guessed by now, it's about a cat, a three-legged cat. A black, three-legged cat.

Tripod was originally owned by a lovely family in the city. They had three elementary school children that took care of him. Tripod was never allowed to leave the yard, but he did. He sneaked out every chance he got!

Children will be children, and they soon tired of caring for him.

My husband acquired Tripod, and I took him to the veterinarian for shots. The vet was very curious and x-rayed his right front shoulder. He found the fourth leg. It was there, but never came down. The tiny skeletal figure of Tripod's right leg was all folded up inside him. This sometimes occurs because mama kitties have too many babies in their tummies and they are crowded. Therefore, there's not enough room for all the kittens to develop properly.

We brought Tripod home from the vet's office on a rainy day, and he seemed to welcome staying in the house. He didn't seem to eat very much. We were soon to find out why. Tripod stole—everybody else's food in the neighborhood. I was told he had even been seen stealing food from the vicious dog's dish up the road. Tripod's successful theft of food from the dog's dish and the fact that he sprayed the area when he left all but destroyed the dog's reputation. This story about that vicious dog does not end here. There is another very embarrassing chapter in this mixed-breed German shepherd's life.

Our white female Manx cat with royal blue eyes had a litter of very vocal, meowing kittens. They were always ravagingly hungry and forever gobbling. Now Tripod heard this ruckus and acted like he wanted to go in the Kitty Castle and see them. We let him in; he went straight to the kittens and Mom. He rolled a kitten over onto its back with all four feet rapidly pawing the air. It was screaming. This was much to April's (Mama Kitty's) dismay, and she quickly popped Tripod on his nose. Tripod left the Kitty Castle, sat on the horse rail, and pouted. Although this was his favorite spot, it was also a good vantage point.

Through the ivy I saw the German shepherd enter our yard. BIG MISTAKE! Tripod jumped off the horse rail and took his stand in the middle of the driveway. He reared back on his hind legs, stretched his one good front paw high in the air, and brought it down on the tip of the dog's nose. NASA couldn't have made a more direct hit! The dog did a 360-degree turn and screamed all the way out of the driveway. We never saw him in our yard again.

Tripod became king after that and dominated the neighborhood for some fifteen years. He had his favorite spots underneath various trees and was never disturbed.

There are no streetlights on our road, and it is always dark at night. My neighbor had worked overtime and was coming home at an odd hour. I heard the squawling of brakes. I grabbed my bathrobe; I just knew it was Tripod. You might well have guessed, it was midnight.

Tripod, being a lady's man, had escorted a lady kitty across the road. She made it and he didn't. The emergency vet's diagnosis was not good . . . Tripod was bleeding from the nose and had a detached brain . . . sometime it is best to let go and that is what we did. If Tripod had lived, he would have had epileptic-like seizures over and over.

Our mighty warrior is buried under one of his favorite trees.

I am beginning to believe that Tripod still dominates the area because I have never seen another cat sleep underneath "his" tree.

Life is s t r a n g e.

*   *   *

Handsome and April

Handsome and April were two white Manx kittens. They were born in April 1990, were brother and sister, and were given to me by my best friend, Arlene.

Handsome was a stumpy Manx with a stubby tail that was approximately two inches long. He had yellow eyes, was shorthaired, and knew how to strut his stuff! Handsome knew he was handsome and also king of the Kitty Castle.

April was a rumpy Manx; that is, she did not have any tail at all. She had beautiful, royal blue eyes that were very rounded and a short body with a good Manx hump in her back. April was an excellent mama; she would take in all the baby kittens that other mothers disowned and raise them. I never saw her turn any little kitten away. She saved many lives.

Together, Handsome and April became the foundation for our Kitty Castle. The Castle was an enclosed deck with a four-room house built in the center of it. This house had four rooms on the second level; the first floor was the deck floor and always had cardboard boxes with numerous holes cut in them scattered about. Water and food was always available, and some kitties and adults got a little plump!

We were so proud of Handsome and April that we took them to many Household Pets Cat Shows and won a lot of ribbons.

Friends and neighbors thought they were very beautiful also, and after much harassment and henpecking, they finally convinced us to breed them.

Their first litter was stolen and we had to lock the Kitty Castle.

We only bred Handsome and April at Christmas, and their kittens were always sold ahead of time. We had a waiting list.

Handsome became so good at perpetuating the species that we had to section an area off inside the Kitty Castle. Much to his dismay, our Handsome was to spend a good deal of time in the "Lockup." He just couldn't keep his "hands" off the ladies.

We bred Handsome and April for five years and then had them spayed and neutered. My husband's health would not allow him to maintain the Kitty Castle, so I took over all responsibilities. I even lifted the fifty-pound sacks of kitty litter. After a little tutoring, I became somewhat proficient with a hammer and nail(s).

I shall never forget one night . . . my husband, Robert, had to get his gun. This was a small pistol. . . .

We were both awakened in the middle of the night by loud, banging/pounding noises coming from the Kitty Castle. Handsome was growling and screaming, and it sounded like a wild animal was howling. My heavens, what could this be? The Kitty Castle was completely enclosed. We grabbed a flashlight, and we both ran into the Castle. The Lady Kitties were not visible. It is a good thing Handsome was white. In the pitch black dark that is how we quickly found him. He was doing a show of force; that is: his hair was standing straight up and his teeth were showing. He was yowling and hissing, spatting, and even batting. At what?

At first, we couldn't see. We shined the flashlight

here and there. Finally in one of the dark corners of the Castle, we saw a figure. A ball of fur, gray and black and two eyeballs. We also saw something else: This animal was drooling from his mouth.

My husband did not want to shoot the animal, which turned out to be a raccoon. But, sometimes, to save other animals, you have to.

The veterinarian determined that the wild raccoon was in early stages of rabies.

It is a mystery to this day how that raccoon gained entrance to the Kitty Castle. There were no holes anywhere.

Many more stories revolved around Handsome and April and the Kitty Castle. One in particular: Blu and Taco, also Duchess.

My husband was approached at work by a woman who was moving but could not take her Manx cat with her. So, Bob came home with another cat. She was rather plump, but he reassured me she was not going to have kittens. Taco had a litter of three kittens; a gray (or blue Manx), a gold one (or salmon-colored), and a black and white Manx. (Some call these Tuxedo cats because it looks like they are wearing a black tux over a white shirt!) They were all rumpies; that is, they had no tails whatsoever. All of these kittens were beautiful Manx babies.

Taco took two days to give birth to all her kittens, and I knew there was something wrong—an obstruction of some kind. However, it wasn't until two and half months later that a veterinarian diagnosed the problem.

The gold or salmon-colored Manx rumpie was sold to some people who came quite a distance and seemed to care a lot and know what they were purchasing.

I kept the tuxedo (black and white) and also the Blue Manx with such beautiful green crystal eyes. Such magnificent, round, gleaming green eyes I have never seen in any animal. Because the black and white Manx was quiet, dignified, and reserved, I named her Duchess. She was also well mannered.

The other Manx, blue gray with crystal green eyes, was simply named Blu. Blu followed Handsome everywhere he went. We think he thought Handsome was his father. Blu was to live fifteen years and he had a funny little habit: When he was in the house, he used to rub up against my back legs, but only when I was washing dishes at the kitchen sink. None of the other kitties did this. Blu had a very kind, loving disposition and would help the mothers with their babies by playing and keeping a watchful eye. He would step aside and give them his food and lick and clean them also. Handsome would do the same thing. Manx males do not kill the kittens; they help to raise them. Both Handsome and Blu would demonstrate techniques of defense and fighting to small cats. It was delightful to watch this family of Manx and also study them. Gratifying.

Blu was a love and always had a special place in my heart. To this day, I still see his beautiful, crystal green eyes. I still remember every morning when I fed him; I would say: "Hello Blu, how do you do?"

Blu and the Duchess both lived fifteen years. The Duchess died of a stroke, and Blu died of an infection in his intestinal tract. But he was not gone yet.

It was summertime, and I was dressed in shorts. I also had sandals on and this exposed my legs. One of my cats came in the kitchen and rubbed my legs. There was no mistaking that soft fur. So I would not step on this animal, I looked immediately down to see who it was: To my shock and surprise, NOBODY WAS THERE! I will never forget that moment as long as I live. I was so shook up and frightened but all those mixed feelings gave way to being honored. Yes, honored. For me, it was Blu's way of saying: "Thank you—but I am not gone. I'm here, but in a different form of life."

Although I have never believed in ghosts, I'm beginning to change my way of thinking.

As for Taco, she was to live a very short life, approximately five years. I noticed she was losing weight and I took her to the veterinarian. The vet took X-rays. They revealed a metal object, small but triangular-shaped. Some kind of BB from a gun. It was lodged near the heart, and the vet did not know how Taco could have lived this long. A miracle. There was also a tumor.

The kindest move to make here is to let go because Taco could not eat any more. The tumor was all over.

She is gone but not forgotten. I see her sleeping on the back of my couch in my memory.

May God Bless her.

*   *   *

Wicked Witch!

I have talked about and shared just about all the wonderful animal experiences I've had with the lovable, playful, and devoted Manx cats.

Except for one.

My husband came to me one day and said, "You know, we do not have a shiny black Manx cat. I think I will start watching the papers for one." And so he did. A couple of weeks went by, and then one day there appeared an ad in our local, small town newspaper:

"Black Manx kittens . . ." I talked to the lady on the telephone and she seemed a bit apprehensive as she explained, "Well, we have all been feeding them at work. You see, Mama Kitty was abandoned . . . and then she had four kittens. One was so small . . . it had no tail at all. She's so cute."

I got an uneasy feeling that I wasn't being told the entire story.

I drove as fast as I could across town in five o'clock traffic. The lady greeted me at the door and said, "Is that your pick-up truck I see out there? We don't allow those vehicles in this area. But, I suppose it won't hurt anything; you'll only be a few minutes. I hope you brought a wire cage and not a cardboard box." I explained, "Yes, I have this wire cage, but the spring on the lid is a little weak. It was built to hold wild animals." The lady explained. "That should do. Follow me to the garage."

Some of the characters from Kitty Castle.

Goldie and Paleface

Tom and his girlfriend

Snowball

The garage would hold four cars and the lights were not too bright. The electrician was not finished. The lady explained, "The kitten is between the wall and the hot water tank in that corner. Lots of luck." She closed the kitchen door behind her as she left the garage. There were empty cardboard boxes scattered here and there plus miscellaneous items in random places. The house-keeper had left but didn't finish cleaning the area.

I looked in the dark corner between the hot water tank and the wall and saw nothing. I did not hear anything either. I wondered if there was a kitten back there. I called, "Kitty, kitty, kitty." That got me nothing also. My uneasy feeling was getting worse.

I knew something bad was going to happen. It did.

I put my hand ever so carefully into the dark, fore-boding corner and felt around for this little kitten. Noth-ing. Again, I called, "Kitty, Kitty, Kitty." I shouldn't have done that! I should have listened to my mother who taught me never to put my hands where I could not see. Because, the third time I called: "Kitty, Kitty, Kitty", I was attacked. Attacked with the velocity and force of a wild, ferocious animal. There were no growls, snarls, or hisses of any kind. No warnings.

Just a surprise attack of an uncountable number of sharp, needlelike claws locking onto my hand and arm. The kitten's back feet came into play and I believe I was bitten as well several times. Growls and snarls followed this attack. I did not pull my arm away but managed to invert it; that is, turn this hissing/spattering ball of fur upside down and lift and drag the wild cat out of the cor-ner. I succeeded.

With my left hand, I grabbed this shiny black kitten by the nape of the neck. It is unbelievable what happened next: She twisted her head and bit my wrist area.

I dropped her and in the dimly lit garage, I chased her round and round and round—over the cardboard boxes, occasionally putting my foot in one and falling head over heels. I was losing the battle when, the lady opened the kitchen door. Out of nowhere sprang the Wicked Witch and she ran into that kitchen.

We had her cornered or so we thought.

I was right on the kitten's heels with a cardboard box and the wire cage, both of which I grabbed on the run.

The lady managed to kick the little animal and knock her against the wooden cabinet. She grabbed the cardboard box out of my hand and stuffed this half-dazed stick of dynamite in it. In a split second, a black paw and arm thrust upward out of the center of the box. I grabbed the wire cage and opened the lid. It was easy because the spring was weak on the latch.

The Wicked Witch was running in circles and round and round the kitchen. Underneath the kitchen table and chairs, and also, between our legs. She made a fool out of both of us. This little animal was not to be conquered.

I had an idea. I told the lady, "Distract her." She did. I dropped the wire cage on top of this wild ball of black fur. The kitten thrust her paw up through the bottom of the cage. I grabbed it and managed to invert the cage, slam the lid closed and latched it. I hadn't taken half of a deep breath, when I saw the Wicked Witch half out of the wire cage. The lady screamed. This was the most intelligent, and the strongest animal I had ever encountered. I grabbed both front legs and that got me bit again and hissed at. I didn't care. I told the lady, "Find some wire!"

She handed me some wire and with my foot on top the cage, I wired the cage closed. The kitten hissed, snarled, and growled at us. She banged her head and body against the cage but could not get out.

We had won.

I was in tears, but I was laughing. The lady was laughing, but also, she too, was crying. It took us almost two hours to capture the Wicked Witch.

My hands and arms were bleeding and bloody. Never in my life had I incurred such injuries from any animal, let alone one that weighed less than four pounds. It took all my skill to catch her.

The lady helped me to wash my hands and arms, put some makeshift bandages on, and pick up the pieces. I was shaking all over. The kitten was in the wired shut cage—snarling.

The lady helped me to my pickup truck, and we loosely covered the wire cage with a piece of black plastic. Darkness quiets animals. But not this one.

Wicked Witch Redux

I arrived home and my husband met me at the gate. I was still shaking. He opened the gate for me. I could see the wondering, "where have you been" look on his face.

I explained, "We had a problem getting her in the cage."

My husband said, "I will help you introduce her to the other animals in the Kitty Castle." I never said a word. NOT ONE!

He unloaded the cage and took it into the Kitty Castle. Instantly, the other Manx cats gathered around, keeping a couple feet of distance between them and the cage as if they knew. The Wicked Witch would not come out of the wire cage. She just looked around. Her presence went over like a lead balloon. The female Max cats hissed and growled at the Witch. Handsome, our white Manx, stood in one place and studied her. When he saw a female cat about to attack her, he would stand between the two. This would end the fight.

Since it was Christmas/Holiday time, Handsome was in with the females preparing for Christmas kittens. This means that his special enclosure was empty. My husband quickly closed the cage and took the Witch to Handsome's enclosure. And, there she stayed for one whole year.

When I went into Handsome's enclosure to feed her, she just backed up in a corner and would hiss and spit at me. I told my husband, "You feed her." The Witch seemed to like my husband much better than me. He fed her.

I could see Handsome not only wanted back in his enclosure but also was curious about The Wicked Witch. One day I let him in with her. She would have nothing to do with him. He had a time of it. Round and round the cage he chased her. There were toys and cardboard boxes and wooden boxes here and there, but he always seemed to know where she was hiding. I did not believe he would successfully breed her. He did. She only had three kittens and one died. The kittens were white, and they were Manx. After that, I had her spayed.

After that first year, I was able to pet the Witch. The other Manx cats carefully accepted her, and she was allowed into the house. She sat on my husband's lap first and became his pet.

The Wicked Witch was to live only eight years. She died of diabetes. However, she, too, will remain in my heart forever.

As for my arms, it took almost six months for them to heal. Some of the scars will never go away.

One Eye

After Tripod died, I missed him very much. I wanted another cat with only three legs, and one day I found myself in the local animals shelter looking for just that. I asked the clerk, "Do you have cat with three legs?" He said, "No, but I have a cat with one eye." I thought for a second and then I said, "Well, let's go take a look."

We did not go to the Cat Room where all the cats/kittens were kept. The clerk took me to a small cage outside that Cat Room: ISOLATION!

When I asked him why she was being kept out here, the clerk responded quickly, "The other cats and kittens do not seem to get along with her, and they pick on her." He slowly opened the small cage door and a seemingly well-mannered one-eyed half-grown cat emerged gently from the cage. She looked all around with a somewhat tilted head. One Eye as she would later become known, was a gray and black tiger stripe with one yellow eye. The right eye was gone, and the eyelid was sewn shut.

The clerk winced when I picked up One Eye and put her on my lap. I petted and talked to her and she purred. I then asked the clerk, "What happened to her eye?" The man responded, "I do not know, and neither does the animal control officer that found her. She was found running down a road that led directly to a six-lane freeway where the speed limit is sixty-five, but drivers go eighty to one hundred out there. The Humane Officer pulled off the road ahead of the animal, who was skinny, dehydrated, very dirty, panting, and had patches of fur missing. She was also bleeding and her eyeball was hanging out. The only reason why the Officer caught this animal is because she was exhausted. The depleted animal was taken directly to a veterinarian and emergency surgery and treatment were started. She was also spayed and given shots. One Eye was adopted twice, and twice she was returned to the shelter."

I knew I was dealing with an animal damaged both emotionally and physically. Somehow, somewhere, this animal was in a horrific fight. She had won. I adopted her on the spot.

Any animal who fought this hard for her life deserves a chance. I knew it would not be easy. It took almost six months, and she broke down several times. She seemed to be afraid of hands. So, that is the spot I started to treat: fear of human hands. I did not put hand lotion on my hands. I put tuna fish oil on them. This seemed to help, and eventually she stopped hissing and batting at me. As for other cats, nobody would accept One Eye. They would block her movement, hiss, and push her off into a corner. Needless to speak of the bizarre stares eyeballs to eyeball. The yowling was worse than any coyote or wild animal. Finally, I removed One Eye from the Kitty Castle. She had rebelled and was fighting with all the other cats and kittens.

Back in the house she came. One Eye hid under the bed, behind the couch, and anyplace else you could imagine. Even in the cupboard under the kitchen sink and the closet. When it got cold she would shimmy underneath my bedspread, and there would be this bump on my bed.

Time passed and I believe One Eye started to relax a little. Months had passed. I didn't let her outside very often. She would pounce the prize neighborhood tomcat, who had never been neutered. He thought he was something, and he made himself known to One Eye. She made mincemeat of him. After that, he made a wide circle around her. What a cat.

One cold, winter night—a breakthrough. I awoke to warm feet, and a weight on them also. I looked down to see One Eye, curled up and sleeping on my feet. After that, she gave me the honor of sleeping in my lap. She had adopted me. Our relationship excelled, and I began letting her outside more and more. She began disappearing. I was worried. But, she always came home to eat and thank me. She also returned home one day with an eight-year-old boy. My neighbor's. He said, "I love your cat. She sits on my lap and lets me pet her. I feed her, too. What happened to her eye?"

I told the little boy all that I knew about One Eye. It was actually the little boy who named her "One Eye." My neighbor boy wanted to have her, but his father would not allow it because they had hunting dogs. I told him he could visit anytime he wanted to.

One Eye had become one of the best mousers and rat catchers I have ever owned. She climbs trees in split seconds and races across the yard. She digs holes in my lawn and garden and hardly ever fails to get gophers, moles, and various other pests. No more do my tomato plants get pulled down a hole in front of me in broad daylight until they disappear!

Occasionally, if One Eye manages to get in a corner, she gets a little confused—so, I have to physically turn her around and help her out. Other than that, she is a normal cat who functions quite well. One would never know she's blind in one eye until she turns around. As for the rest of the "tribe" (that is, my other cats), they finally accepted her, but only to a degree. They eat and play chase in the yard but have never slept together. Maybe some day.

God bless One Eye. She made it.

*   *   *

Grammy Grumps: Our Scottish Fold Story

Scottish Folds, as the story goes, originated in the remote farmlands of Scotland. A farmer saw that a few of his kittens had folded down ears, but he was kindhearted and also very busy. The cats bred at their own will, and soon there was a new breed. Some city people got lost and stumbled across these cute but small folded-eared cats. The farmer was only too happy to give them a few. Officially, a new breed was established.

Scottish Folds eventually found their way to America and also into our hearts.

*   *   *

This story is dedicated to Smoky, our first Scottish Fold. She lived only a few years and died of cancer. God bless her.

My husband saw a cat with folded ears and thought that it was kind of cute. This kitten had a rounded face with beautiful round eyes similar to that of a Manx cat.

I surprised him on his birthday by giving him a Scottish Fold kitten. She was a smoky gray color and very small. We named her Smoky.

We introduced her to the Kitty Castle and, of course, to Handsome. He was very quick to make his masculine presence known, and it wasn't long before Smoky had her one and only litter. She had two white Scottish Fold kittens. One had blue eyes and the other had yellow. Smoky died awhile later.

My husband, Robert, thought the white Scottish Fold kittens were beautiful and kept one. She was grumpy and that is how he named her: Little Grumps.

One day, Little Grumps was in the house and my husband picked her up and sat her on his lap for the first time. She very politely, and with speed of lightning, promptly and quickly bit him on his hand and sunk her teeth in to the gums.

There was no reason for this attack.

He quickly put Grammy Grumps back out in the Kitty Castle. She remained there for ten years and would never come to anybody. My husband passed away never knowing the cause. She never came into season and never had any kittens, until one day I grabbed her up when she was least expecting it and took her to the vet for some overdue shots. I warned the veterinarian, "She bites. She's a pill." I could see him studying her. I went out to wash clothes and took my cell phone with me. It wasn't too long that the vet called and said; "Grammy Grumps has some rotten teeth. Do you want me to pull them?" I said, "Yes." The teeth were pulled and Grammy was taken home. She was a new animal. Her disposition was that of a mellow, purring, lovable animal.

Handsome was quick to pick up on Grammy's new, lovable personality change. After ten years, Grammy Grumps had her first litter. Two white Scottish Fold females—one had blue eyes and the other a crystal yellow.

I sold the yellow-eyed Scottish Fold and kept the blue-eyed one. I named her Pixie because she was mischievous. The yellow-eyed Fold found a good home with a friend of mine and he named her Pixel because she was so small. To this very day Richard loves Pixel and she has everything. Richard and I write back and forth and he sends me photographs. Very beautiful photographs. Pixel lives like a queen!

Pixie was so small, I was afraid to spay her. Little did I realize how watchful the beautiful golden tomcat, Tinker, was. Before my kitchen window, in my own yard! He bred Pixie.

Pixie had three very beautiful kittens: a short white hair with beautiful blue eyes—male, a long white hair silver tabby-male, and last but not least—a smashed golden/white female kitten.

They were born on April 8 and on my bed inside a cloth pyramid bed. You might know at two in the morning! But, no gold one? I knew there would be a gold one. I just knew. I kept shining the flashlight but no gold kitten. On a hunch, I picked up mama Pixie and there was a smashed golden kitten. This little soul was bigger than the two boys and fat. I found her in the nick of time and introduced her to mama Pixie. Little Goldie gobbled milk. In fact, she always ate like a piggy.

I kept the golden Scottish Fold and named her Goldie. Goldie had very long, fluffy hair and copper eyes. She had a white chest and white undercoat. She, too, was very beautiful. I had both Pixie and Goldie spayed, also Grammy Grumps (Little Grumps).

Today, Pixie with her white coat and beautiful blue eyes, Goldie with her magnificent four-inch-long coat and oh, so golden color, and, of course, Grammy Grumps all live together in the Kitty Castle and my house, too.

We are a family.

*   *   *

31

Many Toes . . .

". . . Many toes, my Many Toes, how I loved my Many Toes. Many Toes had many toes and many toes had she . . ."

Indeed, Many Toes did have many toes. The veterinarian counted some twenty-three to be exact. Her front paws looked like furry pancakes! But, we did not care; we loved her. I loved her so much that I wrote the song "Many Toes" and had it put to music.

My girlfriend Arlene was going to give this tiny kitten to her crochety old neighbor, but he did not like her. She was so small, we did not know whether she would live or not. At six weeks, she sat in my left hand, and it felt like she didn't even weigh a pound. In fact, it felt like nothing was there.

Toes was a gray and black tiger-striped kitten with a white spot between her eyes. She had big beautiful rounded eyes, a good Manx hump in her back, and just a tiny bump for a tail.

Many Toes' mama kitty was bitten by a dog, and it left her with a hip injury. The hip would slip out of its socket. Arlene and the vet would replace it and everything would be alright for awhile. I brought my Many Toes (as she was later named) home in a small shoe box that I placed on the floorboards of my pick up truck, passenger side. I carefully and slowly drove the winding mountainous roads home. Many Toes never meowed once, never whimpered, and never cried. In fact, you would never have known that there was a kitten in that box.

I got home and carefully carried the small shoe box into the house, put it on the floor and opened it up. Surprisingly, Many Toes was in the same position in the box that I put her in. She had not moved. She did not jump out of the box; I had to lift her out.

I quickly put fresh water, soft kitten food, and kitten kibble down for her to eat. She did not eat. I had to put drops of water and milk on the tips of my fingers and teach her how to eat. I would make a mush of kibbles and kitten milk. Again, I had to teach her to eat that, too. Many Toes still did not meow. She was very well mannered, though, never scratched my couch, and was not destructive. She loved to play catch and would bring the ball back to me just like a dog. Although Many Toes used the kitty box, every once in a while she would make a mistake.

I was sitting on the couch, which had covers on it. Thank heaven! It was summertime, and I had shorts on. Many Toes had bonded with me and was crowded next to my bare leg when . . . I felt a warm but wet feeling on my bare leg. I looked down in time to see not only a wet spot but this soft stool as well. My husband had to open the front door and kick the fan on high. That was the rottenest, most odoriferous little pile of kitten feces (poop) that I ever cleaned up in my life. I took it to the vet along with Many Toes for her first shots. It turned out that Many Toes is a polydactyl-footed animal—that is, an animal with extra toes. We didn't care; we loved her anyway.

Along with the veterinarian's special feeding instructions, and some special kitten food from his office, Many Toes started to grow. But still no meow. We introduced her to the adults in the Kitty Castle—i.e., Handsome and April. They knew how to meow.

But, alas, still no meow. I carried Many Toes around in my apron pockets and when she got old enough, her head would pop out. She would follow me around the house and I raised her underfoot. I did not think Many Toes would ever grow up at all. I was so afraid she would catch cold at night that I took her to bed and she slept on my face!

One day, when she was half-grown, I clapped my hands to determine whether or not she could hear.

To my surprise, and this is something I will never forget as long as I live. Many Toes did the legendary: a Manx backwards flip.

She only flipped herself about two feet off the ground but in a perfect backwards circle and landed with all four feet on the ground at once.

She looked at me and I looked at her. I believed that we were both in shock at that time.

I took Many Toes into the house and checked her over. She seemed to be alright. I never clapped my hands again. One day Many Toes tried to meow in the form of a squeak, but that is all I ever got before she was stolen.

By now, my beloved polydactyl-footed Many Toes was full grown into a beautiful cymric (a long-haired Manx cat) with hair that measured almost four inches long. She was beautiful.

It was Christmas and many people came to our home to buy our white Manx kittens. I was so busy. I noticed Many Toes was gone. I called and called, searched and searched; but I never found her. All the joy, all the laughter, now tears.

Then one day I had to pick up some kittens in the

city. The directions led me to a wealthier part of this community.

I picked up the kittens and just so happened to see a swimming pool through a fenced area.

The lady who gave me the kittens explained, "That is my neighbor's pool. She loves to swim. The cat is a Manx. They do not have any tails. My neighbor loves her. She's an old lady."

It's my Many Toes. I was in tears but I never explained why. The lady asked me, "What is wrong?" I said, "Nothing, I used to own a Manx cat."

It was plain to see that Many Toes had a wonderful home—so many things I could not give her. I never went back to that part of the City and some fifteen years have passed. It was just too painful.

As for Many Toes's mama kitty, she lived. But, every once in a while her hip would slip out of joint.

I will always love my Many Toes. Arlene moved away and I lost all track of her. . . . and that is the way of life sometimes.

*   *   *

Lady and the Horse Trailer

My husband, Robert, and I were also members of the Sheriff's Posse Volunteer Unit. We not only rescued lost and injured people, but animals as well.

I expected to rescue animals from all parts of the county but never in our own Sheriff's Posse yard. That is exactly what happened.

Our Posse yard was an approximate five-acre area which housed a two-story older home, stalls and corrals for horses, and parking spaces for pick up trucks and horse trailers. Sometimes people would go on vacation and the horse trailers would not be used for awhile.

I was not only feeding my horse but caring for others, and this took a bit of time. I noticed the same beige, slim, rather depleted-looking cat coming and going. Then, he or she disappeared. I temporarily forgot about that cat until one day I heard "meow, meow, meow, meow meow . . ." I followed these faint little repetitive cries to one of the older, least used, junky horse trailers. And there is where I found a mama kitty with three *beautiful* baby kittens. Somehow or another, I just wasn't surprised. Mama kitty had beautiful blue eyes, and was the depleted cat I saw coming and going.

The whole trick to getting mama kitty in the kitten transport cage was to put the kittens in first. Their eyes were not open yet, and their umbilical cords were visible. All three kittens fit in my left hand. Carefully I placed them in the transport cage. Mama Kitty followed automatically.

Handsome was kicked out of his separate stall, and we placed the stray mama kitty with babies in there. She was named Lady and her kittens grew. Lady was attentive, gentle, loyal, and kind. She never left her babies. She was also starving when we got her.

We fed her three times a day and carefully saw to it that she always had water and kibbles. She gobbled and gobbled. Her kittens grew up to be beautiful silver tiger striped, and two had blue eyes.

My husband placed an ad in the local newspaper for homes and a registered nurse and her adopted daughter came and took two of them. A father and son adopted the third. Lady was spayed and lived her life out here as an outside "mouser," until she, too, was adopted by a neighbor.

Happy endings do happen!

*　　*　　*